CONFERENCE PROCEEDINGS

RAND

Conflict and Consensus in Ethno-Political and Center-Periphery Relations in Russia

Edited by Jeremy R. Azrael and Emil A. Payin

RAND Center for Russian and Eurasian Studies
Center for Ethnopolitical and Regional Research

Preface and Acknowledgments

This volume contains translations of studies by four Russian specialists on ethno-political and center periphery relations in the Russian Federation. Fuller versions of these studies are being published simultaneously in a Russian-language volume containing additional studies by other Russian specialists.[1]

Both of these volumes, as well as two preceding volumes entitled, *U.S. and Russian Policymaking With Respect to the Use of Force*, Santa Monica, Calif.: RAND, CF-129-CRES, 1996, and *Cooperation and Conflict in the Former Soviet Union: Implications for Migration*, Santa Monica, Calif.: RAND, CF-130-CRES, 1996, are products of a multi-year collaboration between RAND's Center for Russian and Eurasian Studies and the Center for Ethnopolitical and Regional Research in Moscow.[2] This collaboration, in turn, has been part of a broader RAND project, sponsored by the Carnegie Corporation of New York, to further the development of independent policy-analytic capabilities in Russia.

The studies were singled out for publication in the present volume both because they provide particularly good examples of the theoretical approaches and analytical methods that characterize contemporary Russian scholarship on ethno-political and center-periphery relations and because they focus on issues that rank high on the agendas of relevant Russian (and, in some cases, non-Russian) policymakers. Although these principles of selection have led to the omission of other studies that are of great interest from other perspectives (and are available in Russian), they accurately reflect the priorities that have consistently guided us throughout our personal and institutional collaboration.

We thank the Carnegie Corporation of New York for having made this collaboration possible and the many colleagues who have worked with us for having made it both pleasurable and productive.

Jeremy R. Azrael, Director
RAND Center for Russian and Eurasian Studies

Emil A. Payin, Director
Center for Ethnopolitical and Regional Research

---

[1] The Russian-language volume is entitled, *Evolutsiya vzaimootnoshenii tsentra i regionov Rossii: ot kohfliktov k poisku soglasiya*, Progress, Moscow, 1997.

[2] These latter volumes have also been published in Russian-language editions. See, Azrael, J.R., E.A. Payin, and A. Popov, eds., *Kak delaetsa politika v SShA i Rossii*, Progress, Moscow, 1996; and Azrael, J.R., E.A. Payin, and V. Mukomel', eds., *Migratsiya v postsovietskom prostranstvye: politicheskaya stabilnost' i mezhdunarodnoye sotrudnichestvo*, Progress, Moscow, 1997.

Contents

Tables

1. Typologies of Regional Conflicts in Modern Russia

*Leonid.V. Smyrnygin**

Social development is impossible without contradictions and conflicts. To dream about getting rid of them is not just naive—it is dangerous and harmful because it demobilizes the society and engenders bitter disappointment in the state authority which is incapable to provide development without conflicts. Such dreams are typical for many nations in the world; however, as a rule, they are less common among peoples who have organized their societies along democratic lines. Democracy obliges its citizens to view conflicts as normal, to understand that the solution of one type of conflict takes the society to a new level, which is higher than the previous one but which also abounds in conflicts, albeit of a different kind. It seems that without such a perception of conflicts, democracy does not function—if only because a polity based on the choices of citizens who expect the state to do away with the conflicts once and for all is inherently unstable.

Alas, Russia is not one of the countries whose culture views conflicts as normal. On the contrary, Russian culture tends toward eschatology, toward a deep-rooted belief in the Divine Kingdom on Earth, a land of milk and honey, etc. This is accompanied by a belief that the Kingdom can only be attained at the cost of enormous efforts by the entire population simultaneously. Moreover, it is typical to think that it is only for the sake of this promised land that any public effort should be undertaken. This serves as the basis for the success of politicians such as Zhirinovsky, who "specialize" in making promises, and receive a great many votes—even though the unrealizable nature of their promises is obvious to the majority of those voting for them.

Regional Conflicts

The inevitability of conflicts is especially obvious in the regional context. At its basis lies a deep-rooted contradiction between the interests of the whole and the interests of individual parts. That which is advantageous to the country as a

---

* The author is a member of the Presidential Council of the Russian Federation and a Docent in the Geography Department of Moscow State University.

whole may not always be advantageous to one of its regions, and vice versa. A typical example is environmental protection vs. nuclear energy development. Everyone wants the benefits of power from nuclear plants, but public opinion in any given region opposes building facilities in that region. On the other hand, each region is interested in attracting high wage industries that improve the entire economy of the region. As a result, regional authorities have begun to compete with one another, offering such industries preferential treatment and privileges. In doing so, they often prevent optimal placement from the point of view of benefits to the country as a whole.

Similar disputes can take on far more severe forms leading to distortions in the territorial structure of a country, and even to threats to its integrity. Under uncontrolled market conditions economic players avoid placing enterprises in less developed regions in favor of more developed regions. As a result, poor regions become even poorer, and rich ones still richer, tearing at the economic fabric and political integrity of the country. There are mechanisms in a market economy which soften this process—for example, the constant exchange of labor and capital between regions—but these mechanisms work slowly, and their short-term effectiveness is problematical.

Political leaders, including those in Russia, are constantly faced with a difficult choice: if they stimulate the economic growth of the country, interregional disproportions grow; if, in their opinion, these disproportions are too great and need to be leveled, they must sacrifice economic growth in the more developed/productive regions (where the return on investment is high) to increase the amount of capital investment in less developed regions where the return is lower.

Is the Regional Structure of Russia Truly Stable?

Interregional conflicts, which had decreased in the 1970s–1980s, began to grow faster at the beginning of *perestroika* and intensified sharply thereafter. In particular, the momentum of the USSR's disintegration brought Russia's integrity into question.

However, several factors interfered with the growth of moderated interregional antagonisms in Russia. Russia, as a country, has a rather monotonic physical geography—its parts differ from each other much less than one would expect, given the vastness of the territory (especially if moving latitudinally, where the majority of Russian settlements are situated). Russia is also culturally homogeneous; Russians who live thousands of kilometers from each other differ surprisingly little in their value systems and political cultures. The ethnic diversity of the Russian Federation is far less than it was in the USSR: almost half of the USSR's population was non-Russian; in present-day Russia that number is only 17 percent by ethnicity (and by language, 7-8 percent). As such, Russia looks like a Russian country with a sprinkling of non-Russian enclaves—a country where the "nationality problems" are relatively manageable.

The major binding factor in Russia is the political tradition of state centrism, fostered since the time of Ivan Kalita, and firmly ingrained in the consciousness of the Russian people. The threat of regional separatism had never been an issue for Russia (with the exception, perhaps, of the notorious Polish question), and the threat of disintegration in the 1980s and 1990s was due not to the aggrandizement of power by the regions, but to the weakening of central authority. However, the momentum of centrism was sufficient enough to avoid this danger by 1994.

Standard Regional Disputes in Russia

It is customary to single out four standard types of disputes in any country's territorial structure: between the center and a region, between the regions; between the center and several (or all) of the regions; and the opposition of a single region to the country's regional system as a whole. The severity *ratio* of these categories is different for every country. The same is true for Russia. The disputes which stand out there are found, so to speak, along the vertical axis—between the center (at the federal level) and a region—practically every one of the regions.

Verticality is generally a characteristic feature of Russian culture on many levels, even including religion (suffice it to compare the familiar "horizontal" attitude of a Protestant toward God to the extremely respectful, humble, upwards view of God in the Russian Orthodox faith). In the regional sphere, all disputes seem to be reduced to this verticality. Even when horizontal disputes arise between regions, they take on an entirely vertical form, as the leaders of contending regions or their citizens launch their appeals first to Moscow instead of to each other. Until recently, there was no direct political contact between the regions.

The extreme weakness of horizontal regional relationships reflects the disastrous state of the Russian territorial structure. Contact between neighboring areas is partial and intermittent; the inhabitants, as a rule, are poorly informed about the events taking place nearby, and, moreover, they show no interest in them. These kinds of communications are a little livelier in Siberia and in the Far East, but in European Russia regional self-isolation is very prevalent. Regional borders, as a rule, are overgrown with woods; highways terminate at them, making them easy to distinguish even from satellite photographs. Nothing similar exists in any other developed country. It is because of this that the territorial fabric of Russia, woven only from vertical communications, is thin and precarious. To keep it intact requires the urgent activation of horizontal communications.

Disputes between the center and several regions are fairly widespread abroad, often threatening the territorial integrity of a state. However, they are rare in Russia. We could say "fortunately do not exist," except that the reason for their scarcity is unfortunate due to the aforementioned weakness of contact between neighboring regions. It is true that in Russia, eight regional associations which unite the leaders of neighboring subjects of the Federation have been in existence for six years. Foreign experts assign them a great deal of importance and write about them frequently—far more often than Russian authors. This is with good reason, as it is clear to any Russian analyst that these associations are an artificial political invention. Ostensibly, they were created to coordinate efforts in socio-economic development, but, in reality, they are a concerted effort to extract additional power and funds from the federal authorities and do not assume any political functions. Remarkably, the federal authorities not only did not fear the creation of such associations, but tried to promote their development in every possible way. I have had a number of opportunities to participate in discussions about the possibility of transferring some part of federal powers and concerns not just to the regional level, but first to the interregional level—that is, to the associations. According to Kremlin analysts, this would have regulated the flow of funds and administrative functions from the center outward, expanded the regional strategies of the center, and stimulated cooperation between the subjects of the Federation. Alas! Each one these attempts failed. The associations' leaderships refused to assume any additional responsibilities above and beyond those which the individual members of the association already possessed.

Thus, the associations did not succeed in evolving into comprehensive political structures. To this day, they basically play a decorative role, articulating only interregional interests and possessing no capability to realize them. The interests of the regions that make up the associations proved too diverse; the leadership of each was too absorbed by their own internal problems. Moreover, it is evident that disputes of the "region vs. region" type were forced to the surface here; the associations were amplifying disputes between their participants which would have remained latent had it not been for these associations in the first place.

At the end of 1996, a tendency was emerging to link regions, not by geographic factors, but by other factors. In particular, the mayor of Moscow, Yu. M. Luzhkov, and the governor of Samara, K.A. Titov, have tried to initiate the alliance of "donor regions"—that is, those regions whose budgets did not require federal transfers. The initiators requested that the donors receive certain privileges in the budgeting process. The initiative has been smothered, but it has a future.

The fourth standard type of dispute is one region vs. the regional system, and is expressed by the attempts of a region (i.e., its leadership, entrepreneurs, or public) to improve its position within the regional structure of the country—to achieve unilateral favorable terms, privileges, etc., while using various objective advantages to this end (possession of an unique resource, an especially favorable geographical location, etc.). Conflicts of this sort develop only in the mature stages of the evolution of the territorial-political structure of a country, when regional leaders and organizations become especially aware not only of their interests, but also how to realize them. It is too early to speak about these types of disputes in Russia. Almost all of the appreciable disputes in Russia today are those between the regions and the center. However, when Russia begins to grow economically, regional leaders will start competing with each other to attract investments.

Other Typologies

There are many other classifications of regional conflicts besides the "standard" one. For example, interregional conflicts are often separated by subject matter into: conflicts over resources; territorial conflicts; ethno-cultural and ethno-political conflicts; and so-called "non-realistic" conflicts—all of these are present in Russia today.

Conflicts over resources are especially prominent. First, there are a number of disputes over natural resources, as in the case of the protracted conflict between the governing bodies of the Tyumen *oblast* and the *okrugs* within it that are rich in petroleum and natural gas. More often, there are conflicts over financial (primarily budgetary) resources. The lion's share of the present conflicts among Russia's regions can be reduced to this type. Such conflicts are usually nameless, as the claims of the "deprived" regions are almost always addressed to the federal authorities, and not to those regions who received more than their share; therefore, externally, such disputes do not appear interregional in character.

Conflicts over investment resources, which are so widespread in the West, are much less common in Russia, where there are few interregional investments. Nevertheless, there have already been conflicts of this type. Probably the most vivid example is the disputes between the Stavropol *krai* and neighboring Ingushetia. When the latter obtained the right to establish a free economic zone with considerable tax breaks, many enterprises from Stavropol began registering in Ingushetia. The discontent of the Stavropol leaders was caused by the fact that, in reality, these enterprises remained in the *krai*, and utilized its infrastructure, but their taxes (albeit reduced) were paid to Ingushetia. Such conflicts will increase.

Territorial Conflicts

The most egregious example here is Primorsky *krai*, whose governor, at different times, has made territorial claims on practically all of his neighbors—China, Khabarovsk *krai*, and Sakhalin. However, on the whole, such disputes are usually settled to the mutual satisfaction of both parties, although in each case one of the regions loses a part of their territory. This was the case in 1995, when the Sokolsky district of the Ivanovo *oblast* was transferred to Nizhny Novgorod. The district is cut off from the Ivanovo *oblast* by a wide reservoir while convenient highways connect it to Nizhny Novgorod, many of whose residents have built *dachas* (country homes) there. While the district was a burden to the Ivanovo authorities, it was an asset to the Nizhny Novgorod authorities, and the border negotiations between the two subjects—the first such negotiations in the new Russia—were completed successfully.

Similar negotiations are under way to transfer to two or three Novosibirsk districts to the Omsk *oblast*; these districts are much closer to Omsk than to Novosibirsk. In this case, however, the Omsk administration opposes the transfer because the western Novosibirsk districts are mostly undeveloped.

Ethno-cultural and ethno-political conflicts also exist in Russia, despite the modest percentage of ethnic non-Russians among the overall population. Such conflicts usually have two sides: mutual or unilateral ethnic hostility, and aspirations to political isolation on behalf of one of the groups. Although ethnic hostility is no more widespread in Russia than in other multinational countries, it is frequently the cause of regional conflicts, especially at the borders of national administrative entities. As we know, the administrative borders of the Russian "autonomies" poorly reflect the real distribution of non-Russian peoples; the titular nations, on the whole, constitute less than half of the local population in these "autonomies," whereas about 40 percent of the non-Russian population live outside of their own ethnic "autonomies." It is for this reason that there are periodic appeals to reconsider their borders and disputes about administrative jurisdictions.

The best-known conflict of this type involves the Tatars and the Bashkirs, and many other examples could be cited. However, the number of actual border disputes is insignificant in comparison with their potential number.

Far more widespread are ethno-political conflicts in which national leaders seek to secure political status for "their" nation, or raise the latter's existing political status, and thereby increase their own national influence. For example, M. Shaimiev, the president of Tatarstan, has become one of modern Russia's most influential regional politicians. It is possible to say that he is the only one among them who acts on "equal terms" with Yeltsin at meetings—both public and private. The President of Yakutia, M. Nikolaev, has obtained a large number of privileges for his republic due to his personal contacts with the Russian president. For other Russian regional leaders, both politicians, along with the President of Bashkortostan, M. Rakhimov, have became symbols of the benefits associated with playing the "nationalities card" in politics. At the same time, they have become embodiments of asymetrical relations in the Russian Federation. Such relations, in turn, are a probable source of serious "horizontal" conflicts between Russia's regions, as it is precisely the asymmetry of the federation that has become the main irritant of the mutual relations between its subjects. Most likely, the first conflicts will arise between neighboring regions and will acquire a territorial flavor.

It is not difficult to identify other types of conflicts in the territorial structure of modern Russia. For example, we can take goals as a basis for classification. In Chechnya, the aim is secession; in all other "autonomies" privileges are the objective; in conflicts between the regions and the center the goal is additional rights for one, several, or all of the regions.

It is also possible to distinguish conflicts by their duration, differentiating between the acute, the chronic, and the continuous (so-called "eternal"). Disputes between the federation and the regions belong to the "eternal" category since their roots lie in the intrinsic contradiction between a part (or parts) and the whole. It is impossible to hope for this type of contradiction to outlive itself; it can only be limited, translated to other forms, and softened as much as possible. Ethno-cultural conflicts must be considered chronic for Russia; their resolution requires long-term measures. In particular, it would be extremely dangerous to try to completely equalize the status of the regions and the "autonomies." However, it is possible to assist the evolution of the country's territorial structure in this direction. Finally, it is necessary to stop the acute conflicts as quickly as possible using tactical means.

When designing policies, it is important not to confuse these types of conflicts. The Chechen crisis looks acute because it has become very extreme, and there are many people who wish to end it as quickly as possible. However, this is a chronic crisis that requires patience and caution to settle; the use of quick measures "to put out the fire" can only be detrimental. Another example: the dispute between the Tyumen *oblast* and its *okrugs* has been going on for several years and looks chronic, but, in reality, it is a typical acute conflict whose settlement should not be delayed unnecessarily.

Finally, there is one additional typology of conflicts, and it sheds light on the situation in Russia. This is the division of all conflicts into the categories: urgent, potential, and dormant. From this perspective, it is possible to say that in the Russian territorial structure today there are no urgent conflicts except the Chechen conflict, and that all other conflicts are potential or dormant.

In fact, strictly speaking, *conflict* as a concept can be defined as a dispute which cannot be resolved within the existing legal framework, and which compels the parties to use force. If we are to adhere to this definition, urgent conflicts involve violent actions. In the meantime, the overwhelming majority of regional disputes, which in Russia are called "conflicts," amount only to threats.

A good illustration of this phenomenon are the words of Boris Fedorov, spoken at the end of 1993, when he was Russia's Minister of Finance. He pointed out that, in 1993, there were 37 cases of leaders of federation subjects who, unhappy with the behavior of the federal authorities, threatened to stop making tax payments to the federal treasury. One could say that there were 37 conflicts present here! However, in reality, none of these threats was carried out, if only because the tax collection bodies are not subordinate to the administrative leaders in the *oblasts*. Therefore, even if they could be called conflicts, they would only be classified as dormant, and by no means urgent.

A conclusion inevitably rises: it is necessary to typologize not only the conflicts themselves, but the ways in which they can be resolved or minimized—shifted from an urgent to a dormant phase.

Resolving Regional Conflicts

We should begin with objective circumstances, some of which have been mentioned above. First of all, there is the tradition of the rigid centralization of state life. This engenders many disappointing defects in the political culture of the Russian people, such as a habit of seeing "real authority" only in the leadership of Moscow, making it responsible for everything, and resigning oneself to the tyranny of local authorities. However, this tradition also involves the extreme mistrust of local politicians who lobby for too much regional independence from Moscow. People are naturally afraid that in such cases there is no keeping the local leaders in check. It is permissible for local politicians to scare Moscow with their independent actions, but there are boundaries, and crossing those boundaries puts political careers at risk, especially in the aftermath of the disintegration of the USSR. This strongly limits the regional authorities in their opposition to federal authorities. In addition, the ghost of "the momentum of disintegration" constantly kept the federal authorities in a state of high attentiveness toward eliminating conflicts with the regions.

The means by which the federal authorities dealt with regional conflicts deserve the closest attention. Experience has shown that these means have been highly effective; thanks to them Russia has overcome the immediate danger of disintegration, which at the outset was rather acute.

Analysis allows us to distinguish five kinds of strategies used by the federal authorities. Certainly, we do not mean to suggest that all such strategies were entirely comprehended, expressed in documents, or known to all politicians or the country at large. On the contrary, the major trends consisted of a sequence of tactical steps, taken rather intuitively, and based on medium-term goals. It is worth pointing out that a large role was played by Boris Yeltsin, whose unusual combination of resoluteness in critical moments and extreme caution during quiet periods demonstrated an effective use of his considerable political intuition and skills. He accelerated the institutionalization of federalism because it was the only way to preserve Russia's integrity, not because he was a federalist in principle.

The most obvious strategy of the federal authorities was to minimize the scale of the conflicts; the Kremlin strove to reduce many basic political disputes to specific events in order to resolve them separately. The clearest illustration of this strategy was the bilateral agreements that were made with the subjects of the federation, wherein similar problems facing all subjects were dealt with separately, region by region. Mutual concessions, promises, and guarantees were offered, in many respects, according to the danger posed by a given region's leadership to the tranquillity of the country's regional structure. In many cases, the results of these negotiations have remained hidden from the public. Only the text of the agreements appeared in the press; the substance of the agreements, found in their numerous appendices, remained "behind the scenes."

The inclination to reduce conflicts through "fragmentation" is seen in many other steps taken by the Kremlin and by the Yeltsin himself—in fact, in almost all instances. For example, the President has built his monthly meetings with the governors into a tradition; however, he meets with only with five or six of them at a time, and the governors have to "earn" such meetings by showing loyalty to the federal authorities. Meetings with all the regional leaders simultaneously are extremely rare; even when they have occurred, they have been mainly ceremonial, with no opportunity for the governors to express a collective point of view.

Another discernible strategy involved "stretching time." A textbook example of this tactic is the notorious phrase, "take as much independence as you can swallow." It was said at a time when the federal authorities had practically no power to resist the separatist dispositions of the "autonomies." Yelstin removed the immediacy of the conflict with this slogan, thereby deferring the need for action until a stronger Russian state could speak with separatists on an equal footing. The Kremlin's subsequent strategy was also one of compromise, aimed primarily at avoiding having to make a "cardinal" decision at an ill-suited time.

The third strategy used by the federal authorities was to transform conflicts from one type to another—that is, from the kind that are not easy to resolve to more manageable types. This strategy is very widespread in federalist states. In some ways, federalism itself is a means to such transformations. Much has been written about the longtime practice used in the United States of transferring class conflicts and other social conflicts into territorial or interregional conflicts, because the country has learned to deal efficiently with these conflicts (after the Civil War).

Federalism in Russia has not yet become such an effective weapon. Here we may talk about transforming regional conflicts into other kinds of conflicts. A good example was the severe crisis in Russia's state system in October 1993. There was a danger that the split between the branches of federal authority and the resultant decline of central authority would sharply activate separatist feelings among regional leaders. Thus Russia might have found itself on the threshold of territorial disintegration—or, if we may, "semi-disintegration." However, this did not happen. The breach between the President and Russia's Parliament affected the regions as well, by separating the governors from local legislatures. Thus, the opportunity for the regional leaders to unite was eliminated.

It is possible to suspect that this was not a deliberate strategy or calculated measure on the part of the Kremlin; however, that is absolutely not the case. At that time, practically all of the governors were appointed by the President, and their appointments were constituent upon maintaining their loyalty to him, while the legislatures had a rigid system of vertical subordination, and for this reason they inevitably expressed solidarity with the central Parliament. Therefore, a regional conflict did not occur because it was supplanted by the conflict between the branches of power.

Federal authorities have also come to understand that they can use conflicts to their advantage. In this manner, the contentions between the *okrugs* and the Tyumen *oblast* have been used to raise the importance of the federal authorities as supreme arbiter. The same is true of conflicts between governors and mayors of regional capitals. Federal leaders see mayors as valuable allies in dealing with regional governors, not least because they see the large cities as "bastions" of reform and sources of votes in federal elections.

Finally, it is worth mentioning a strategy which we will call "underfederalism." Contrary to the widespread opinion among foreign Russian "experts," the federalization of Russia has come about primarily on the initiative of the federal authorities, and not at all because of pressure from the various *oblasts* and *krais* (the autonomous republics are a special case). While moving toward federalism, however, federal authorities have been careful to maintain many elements of a unitary state.

The epitome of this underfederalism was the institution of the governors, appointed by the President of Russia. Even after 1997, however, when all governors became elected officials, "underfederalism" was kept alive in many other forms. Many of these forms are well-known, but one requires separate mention since it has been neglected by most analysts.

Since Russia's independence, its regions have achieved considerable financial self-sufficiency; if, previously they accounted for only 45 percent of the consolidated budget (all-Russian plus all regional), now that figure is about 55 percent. However, in reality, the expenditures are in many respects controlled by the Ministry of Finance, and keeping the financial independence of regions in check in this way restricts regional leadership in its opposition to Moscow. Since Stalinist times, there has existed in Russia a so-called common budgetary system, according to which all budgetary departments report to the Federal Ministry of Finance. This means that part of each *oblast's* administration, which seems rigidly subordinate to its leadership, contains one department which receives its salary from the Ministry of Finance—the department of budget administration. Although it acts only on the regional budget, which is composed by other departments of the administration, and voted on by the regional parliament, the employees of this department unquestioningly report to the Ministry of Finance; if the governor's wishes or orders come into conflict with these instructions, all the worse for the governor.

Conclusion

In the past several years the Kremlin has been rather successful in eliminating regional conflicts. However, changes that promise to produce many difficulties, and shock the Kremlin, as well as Russia, are imminent. Regional conflict management, which has been one of the most successful undertakings of "Yeltsin's team," now threatens to become a major source of headaches, beginning imminently.

The main reason for this is not that the federalization of Russia has gone awry, much less that, as some have claimed, it is inherently un-Russian. The main reason is that the federal authorities are not ready to deal with the consequences of freeing regional governors from presidential control. In effect, the rate of federalization has outpaced the ability of the federal authorities to control it. As a result, conflicts which yesterday looked merely dormant or potential are becoming actual and acute.

Disputes, and even conflicts, among Russia's regions are also on the rise and could become quite serious. Paradoxically, however, such horizontal conflicts promote Russia's unity. Thus, the escalating inter-regional struggle for limited investment resources leaves no room for anti-Moscow demagoguery, let alone real confrontation. Such complaints worsen a region's image and indicate a leader's inability to resolve local problems without help, thereby discouraging potential investors and decreasing a region's competitive chances.

A striking example of the renewal of interregional relations is the story of the agricultural bonds, into which a considerable debt (9 trillion rubles) from almost all of the regions to the federal authorities was transferred, and which arose due to the inability of regional authorities to repay loans against the 1996 crop. The Ministry of Finance planned to issue these bonds at a flat initial price, hoping that prices would be self-determined in the secondary market. This was not the case. Potential buyers who submitted their applications to Oneksimbank (the depository), quickly withdrew them as soon as they learned about the flat price. It was clear to them that the risks involved in purchasing the bonds of, for example, the Adygeya and the Sverdlovskij *oblasts*, were absolutely different—consequently, the price should have been different as well. Since the real parity of the risks remained unknown, the buyers simply preferred to avoid making the transactions.

In sum, we are likely to see the aggravation of two types of conflicts: between the center and the regions as a whole; and between the regions themselves. The ways in which these conflicts will evolve will most likely be different. Center-regional conflicts are going to have to be diverted from the budgetary to the purely political sphere if they are to remain manageable, whereas inter-regional conflicts will probably assume a purely economic form. If the conflicts of the first type are replete with serious dangers to the stability of the country's development, conflicts of the second type promise numerous positive consequences—the most important of which is the interaction among regions which has been so lacking in the territorial development of Russian society.

2. Ethnic Separatism

*Emil A. Payin**

Background

Although the Constitution of the Russian Federation does not mention special ethnic-territorial entities, such entities do exist.[1] Autonomous republics, *okrugs,* and *oblasts* were formed and developed as expressions of political self-determination and ethnic self-defense by so-called "titular" nationalities (representatives of ethnic communities lending their names to the appropriate administrative units). Beginning in the late 1980s, titular nationalities became more concentrated in their respective "autonomies" as their share of the total population increased (exceptions are the Khakas, Mariyts, and Mordovian groups in the corresponding republics of Khakasia, Mari El, and Mordovia, and also some smaller indigenous ethnic groups in the autonomous *okrugs* of Siberia and the Far East).[2] Parallel to this, the share of the "non-titular" population groups decreases, as does their number, while their migration from many republics increases. For the period between 1989-1994, the number of Russians decreased in such republics as Kalmykia, Adygeya, Karachaevo-Cherkessia (within 1 percent), Dagestan (3.5 percent), Buryatia (3 percent), Yakutia (more than 11 percent). Needless to say, the most significant reduction in the Russian population (by more than two-thirds) has taken place in the Chechen Republic.[3]

Ethnic Russian emigrants from the newly independent states and the "autonomies" of Russia have relocated largely to the predominantly Russian

---

* The author is Advisor to the President of the Russian Federation on Nationality Problems, and Director of the Center for Ethnopolitical and Regional Research.

[1] In Russia, 89 regions count as subjects of the federation. Each of these falls into one of two basic categories: 1) ethnic-territorial entities, 32 in total (21 republics, 10 autonomous okrugs, and 1 autonomous oblast); 2) administrative-territorial entities, 57 in total (these are the krais and oblasts, populated mostly by ethnic Russians, and the cities of Moscow and St. Petersburg). The term "subject of the federation" was first used following the signing by the representatives of the majority of these entities of the agreement separating regional and federal authority (the so-called Federal Agreement). Two republics, Tatarstan and Chechnya, refused to sign the Federal Agreement.

[2] These conclusions are made on the basis of comparative analysis of the data obtained as a result of the All-Union Population Census of 1989 and the Microcensus of the Population of Russia of 1994, kindly provided to the author by the Statistical Committee of the Russian Federation. So far, there is no data on the population more recent than that provided by the Microcensus of 1994.

[3] Since the microcensus in the Chechen Republic was not conducted in 1994, all conclusions regarding the changes in the population are made on the basis of expert estimates.

krais and *oblasts* of the Federation. Thus, the territorial delineation of the basic ethnic communities of the country has become all the more noticeable. This, in turn has further accentuated the contradictions between the two types of territorial units in the Russian Federation.

The Evolution of Separatism

"The Parade of the Sovereignties"

From 1990–92, the autonomous republics in the Russian Federation followed in the footsteps of republics of the Soviet Union and declared sovereignty. The leaders in this so-called "parade of sovereignties" were Tatarstan, Yakutia, and Checheno-Ingushetia. That "sovereignty" was precisely what was intended is indicated by the new constitution and initial legislation adopted in Tatarstan. In the constitution, the republic was defined as "a sovereign state, subject to international rights" and associated with Russia through a "constitutional agreement" that allowed for unilateral disassociation. In the republic's "Law on Natural Resources," all state property and natural resources located in Tatarstan were claimed as the exclusive property of the republic. The republic's law, "Conscription and Military Service of the Republic of Tatarstan's Citizens," required the citizens of the republic to perform military service only within Tatarstan's borders. Almost identical examples could be cited for the other "autonomous" republics.

The Russian authorities, frightened by the outbreak of armed ethnic conflicts in other former Soviet republics and remembering the failures of Gorbachev's ethno-political policies, were initially very accepting of the declarations of sovereignty by the "autonomies." In fact, the latter's real political weight was increased by the establishment, under Yeltsin's chairmanship, of a council of republican leaders which was supposed to resolve major issues of national policy. This accommodating approach initially had positive results and prevented ethnic bloodshed on Russian territory. By 1993, however, the concessions made by Yeltsin's administration to the "autonomies" became a subject of increasing criticism.

The escalating struggle for power in Moscow frequently failed to take into the account the consequences to state politics, and speculations on the problems of federalism and separatism for inter-political purposes made it increasingly difficult, if not impossible, for Russia to conduct a coherent ethno-federal policy. By the spring of 1993, the confrontation between the parliament (the Congress of

National Deputies and Supreme Soviet of the Russian Federation) and the government (the President and Council of Ministers of Russia) had led to something approaching complete political paralysis. In the course of their struggle, moreover, a tug-of-war began between the parties for the purpose of attracting regional authorities into their respective camps. Understanding the importance of their support, the leaders of the "autonomies" began to ask a higher price for it. Thus, the regional leaders became a "third force" with a stake in the struggle between the two branches of federal authority and an interest in prolonging it.

Taking advantage of the weakness of federal authority, Chechnya, Tatarstan, Bashkiria, and Yakutia stopped all payment of federal taxes, placing the full federal tax burden on the shoulders of the predominantly Russian regions. Similarly, Yakutia demanded and obtained permission to retain 25 percent of the diamonds extracted there, as well as a substantially greater share of profits from the sale of "its" gold. In the political realm, things went so far that the Kremlin almost agreed to incorporate a provision allocating the "autonomies" as many seats in the upper chamber of the Russian parliament as the much larger and more populous Russian *krais* and *oblasts* in the new constitution it was drafting.[4] Furthermore, President Yeltsin agreed that relations between all of the "autonomies" and the federal authorities could be regulated by bilateral agreements of the sort that had been concluded with Tatarstan and Chechnya after the latter refused to sign the Federation Agreement.

Despite these concessions, radical movements in a number of republics in Northern Caucasus, Volga region, and Siberia continued to demand either outright secession or further concessions that directly threatened the integrity of the Russian state. This tendency was most pronounced in the Chechen Republic, where Dudaev's extremist nationalist group seized power and announced the republic's secession from Russia. However, it was also very strong in Kabardino-Balkaria and elsewhere. In fact, in 1992–1993, Russia faced a real threat of a number of republics seceding, which would inevitably have given rise to bloody conflicts. Yeltsin's forcible dissolution of parliament in October 1993 deserves credit for averting this outcome and preventing Russia's possible complete disintegration, whatever its demerits in other respects.

---

[4] The provision was in fact incorporated in a very early draft of the presidential version of the new constitution.

The Search for Consent

The restoration of meaningful central power as a result of the "October events" was undoubtedly an important factor in convincing the majority of regional councils to rescind their decisions to disregard presidential decrees. The firmness displayed by federal authorities in halting extremist actions (for example, in not allowing the capture of government buildings in Kabardino-Balkaria's capital) also drastically reduced ethnic tensions and helped stabilize the political situation. Nevertheless, the main result of the "October events" and the subsequent elections to the Federal Assembly was a decision by both federal and regional authorities to change political tactics and seek compromise.

The 1994 Agreement on Public Accord, and the 1994-95 agreements on the differentiation of jurisdiction and authority between the federal center and a number of republics were milestones in this regard. The agreements with the republics in many cases became the instrument for bringing local laws into conformity with the Federal Constitution. Similarly, it became much harder for republic leaders to pander to secessionist sentiment once they had signed (as all except Dudayev did) the Agreement On Public Accord with its affirmation that ". . . the rights of the Federation's subjects can be realized only if the state integrity of Russia and its political, economic and legal unity is maintained."

One of the first practical expressions of the new concept of "consent" was the agreement "On the Differentiation of Authority Between Various State Agencies of the Russian Federation and the Republic of Tatarstan." The agreement severely weakened the positions of radical nationalist forces in the republic, whose influence was based almost entirely on fear of an "imperial enemy." The agreement between Moscow and Kazan dissipated this fear in Tatarstan, and the radical nationalist movement, which up to that point had been fairly strong, literally fell apart. By late 1993 to early 1994, a similar, though less complete, weakening of separatist tendencies began in the majority of the "autonomies." The continuation and acceleration of this process culminated in the 1995–96 defeat of the separatist forces in local elections in the overwhelming majority of the republics, as well as in the elections to the State *Duma* and the presidential elections. Certainly, it would be incorrect to speak of the elimination of all disagreements between the federal authority and the ethnic republics, because all of the latter still have laws on their books that contradict the Constitution of Russia; and because, in the territory of the Chechen Republic, Russian laws are completely inoperative. However, the threat of Russia's disintegration has undoubtedly decreased for the present, and Chechnya is now alone in claiming independence from Russia.

Future Scenarios

Looking ahead, one can envision a number of mid- to long-term scenarios of ethno-political development.

Scenario 1: Continued Stability

A number of features of political development in Russia distinguish it from the USSR (as well as Yugoslavia and Czechoslovakia), and suggest that it will probably preserve its territorial integrity. Whereas the ruling elites of all of the constituent republics of the USSR sought to free themselves from Moscow's overbearing domination, the leaders of Russia's *krais* and *oblasts* are increasingly resentful of the political privileges of the ethnic "autonomies." Among other things, they remember all too well the enormous difficulties that arose after the breakup of the USSR—the disruption of traditional economic relations, the establishment of customs and political barriers to trade, etc. The regions have also felt the negative consequences of separatism in the Russian Federation itself, where Kalmykia, Dagestan, the Chechen Republic, and some other "autonomies" have made territorial claims to the neighboring Russian *oblasts.* Hence, they strongly favor equality for all subjects of the federation and are determined to preserve the country's territorial integrity.

Leaders apart, the population of the Russian Federation is far more ethnically homogeneous than was the population of the USSR. Russians make up 83 percent of the total population, and between 85–98 percent of the population of over half (49) of the country's regions. Furthermore, the non-Russian population of the Federation is rather non-homogeneous. The majority of it (approximately two-thirds) is comprised of so-called "diaspora" communities (Ukrainians, White Russians, Poles, etc.) that aspire to nothing more than cultural autonomy. Titular nations, residing within the borders of their ethnic territories, make up less than 5 percent of the population of the Federation, and they are the only ones capable of seeking independence from Russia. However, only those titular peoples who make up a majority of the population in the territory of their republics are at all likely to claim independence with any seriousness, and such majorities constitute less than 3 percent of the country's total population and can be found only in the Northern Caucasus (with the exception of Adygeya), Kalmykia, Chuvashia, and Tuva.

Looking at these six cases, Northern Ossetia can be excluded at once because, as the only Christian "autonomy" in the Muslim North Caucasus, it will not want to leave Russia under any readily conceivable circumstances. Secession from the

Federation is also unlikely in the North Caucasus republics that have two or more titular nationalities—Dagestan, Kabardino-Balkaria, Karachaevo-Cherkessia—since the majority of the population realizes that even the suggestion of secession from Russia would invite an explosion of demands for internal secession and of internal conflicts. Finally, Chuvashia is also an improbable candidate since it has no borders with other states and, hence, could be completely blockaded by Russia.

Scenario Number 2: Contagion from Chechnya

Today's Chechnya is, *de facto*, independent of Russia, as neither the Constitution nor the laws of the Russian Federation are enforced on its territory. Federal authorities do not control Chechnya and have practically no influence on its politics. Just the opposite is true: with the opening of the Chechen link in the pipeline that transports Caspian oil from Azerbaijan to the West, it is Grozny that will acquire a dangerous weapon for blackmail and pressure against Moscow. Hence, there is little probability that Chechnya will ever return to the Russian Federation. The question is rather: will an "independent Chechnya" inspire other republics to emulate it?

This might not be a farfetched idea if one could imagine a prosperous, independent Chechnya. In fact, however, the prospects for simply restoring Chechnya's economy in the near future are highly problematic, as are the prospects for political stability. The very conditions that helped the Chechen forces supporting Djokhar Dudaev and his close colleagues achieve military success will interfere with any attempt to establish domestic peace; namely, the existence of military settlements and an armed population. Given the current state of destruction, these particular conditions will lead to increasing criminal activity, both inside and outside the Chechen Republic. Even now, in fact, the level of incursions on neighboring territories is increasing. Although the republic's leaders are trying to stabilize the situation, they cannot sanction those who only yesterday comprised the elite and the nucleus of their own armed forces. Dudaev could not do it, and there is no compelling reason to believe that his successors will be more successful.

The presence of strongly armed and increasingly criminalized armed bands creates insurmountable obstacles to any reorganization plans if the Chechen government poses a serious threat to Chechnya's immediate neighbors, especially the peoples of Dagestan. Under these conditions, anti-Chechen sentiments are growing in the neighboring republics, and the probability that Dagestan or any other republic of the Northern Caucasus will voluntary join

Chechnya or follow in its footsteps is very low. Nor is the Chechen leadership likely to sponsor an invasion of Dagestan in the hope that their forces would be supported by a "fifth column" of similar communities and that Russia would be unable to react effectively. While this eventuality cannot be entirely ruled out, for the foreseeable future the Chechen leadership is likely to be much too preoccupied with domestic issues to think about foreign or irredentist adventures.

Scenario Number 3: Growing Great Russian Chauvinism

In theory, it is possible to imagine political developments that would bring radical nationalists to power in Russia and to the formation of a government that would repudiate federalism and try to abolish all attributes of statehood in the "autonomies." In response to this, strong separatist movements of the non-Russian peoples would reemerge.

The detonator of the outbreak of Russian nationalism could be the discontent of marginal groups among the Russian population, above all in the "near abroad," where the anger engendered by real and imaginary ethnic discrimination against Russians is much higher than it is in the "autonomies" of Russia proper and where a virulent species of Russian nationalist irredentism has already appeared in the Crimea, in Northern Kazakhstan, and in Transdniester. This irredentist nationalism is being actively cultivated by Great Russian chauvinists within Russia and, in connection with the outbreak of ethnic violence in the "near abroad," could help the latter create a powerful mass movement for the "reunification" of all "Russian" lands.

In addition to members of the "Russian diaspora," Russian refugees from zones of conflict (about 1.5 million people, concentrated largely in the conflict-prone area of North Caucasus) could be the source of growing Russian nationalism. Indeed, many refugees already have a radical nationalist orientation. Furthermore, and perhaps even more disturbingly, radical nationalism is also on the rise among the Cossacks, especially among the militarized Cossack formations in the North Caucasus, where they come into direct contact with other armed groups, particularly the Chechens. Thus, in the case of sharp deterioration of ethno-political relations in Russia's neighboring states, or of an increase in the already large refugee flow from conflict-prone Russian "autonomies," one could expect a growth of radical nationalism among both the Russian and non-Russian populations.

It is also impossible to exclude a resurgence of "nomenclature nationalism" under the aegis of members of the former political elite (as a rule, of its second and third echelon) who today are returning to influential posts in the governing bodies in Moscow, and of regional political leaders who have begun to openly express the nationalistic views they concealed when they first came to power in the aftermath of the breakup of the USSR. Both these groups not only share typical Soviet prejudices (against the West, against Jews, Muslims, etc.) but are also pragmatically interested in fanning mass nationalism. Doing so allows them:

- to shift the blame for their own mistakes in governance to their "Gaidarist" predecessors, whom they accuse of having betrayed Russia's national interests for the benefit of the West;
- to lobby on behalf of those businessmen who want state protection from foreign competitors; and
- to defend themselves from criticism on the ground that they are being criticized for being "true to the national idea."

The success of their efforts can be seen in recent surveys which show a significant increase in xenophobia among the supporters of even those political parties and movements which eschew ethnocentrism in their platforms and programs.

Conclusion

The preceding analysis shows that the severity of ethno-political problems in Russia has not really lessened, but that their intensity has varied over time. If the danger of the disintegration of Russia under pressure from the separatist-oriented nationalist movements was quite real between 1991 and 1993, then today the greatest danger is the growth of mass xenophobia as a prelude to the introduction of radical nationalist policies.

3. Budgetary Federalism

*Aleksei M. Lavrov**

The Russian Model of Budgetary Federalism

Independent Russia inherited a highly centralized, unitary budget system from the USSR. Until 1991, republic, regional, and local authorities could not conduct an independent tax and budget policy. Higher authorities "coordinated" the income and expenses of various administrative units and subsequently "combined" them into a single budget. That budget established the division of portions of various categories of taxes for each individual republic or region among local budgets and authorized the financing of approved expenses. If necessary, subsidies or grants were provided which were designated to cover the "scheduled" expenses fully. Tax revenues collected by republic, regional, and local financial agencies—all of which reported to the Ministry of Finance—were dutifully remitted to the central budget fund. However, under the conditions of a deepening crisis, the instability of this system was clearly revealed. The collapse of the USSR became a reality when the former Union republics stopped paying taxes to the USSR.

From 1991–93, the Supreme Soviet of the Russian Federation adopted a number of laws that introduced the main principles of budgetary federalism into Russia's legal system. However, these laws were never enforced. Instead, inter-budgetary relations occurred largely spontaneously as a result of political conflicts and compromises among federal and regional authorities. The republics of Tatarstan, Bashkortostan, Yakutia, etc.—the leaders of the "Parade of the Sovereignties"— virtually stopped paying taxes into the federal budget fund, whereas the majority of the "law-abiding" (more to the point, less influential) subjects of the Federation were still compelled to rely on behind-the-scenes lobbying for favorable rates of federal taxation and for federal subsidies to cover their local budget deficits. This situation was extremely unstable, inducing some regions to attempt to improve their standing in the budgetary hierarchy by behaving like republics, presenting ultimata to federal authorities, making decisions to suspend paying taxes to the federal authorities, and using to their

*The author is Advisor to the Territorial Directorate of the Presidential Administration of the Russian Federation.

advantage any conflicts between various branches of the federal power structure, etc.

This period of "spontaneous decentralization" of the budgetary system was over by the end of 1993. The inter-budgetary reform that occurred in 1994 created a foundation for the Russian model of budgetary federalism that, with insignificant variations, is still in place. Its basic elements are the following: granting subjects of the Federation the right to independently establish tax rates on corporate profits; introducing unified rates for federal allocations to regional budgets; lifting barriers to the introduction of new taxes by local authorities; and creating the Fund for Financial Assistance to the Regions (FFPR) to distribute (transfer) federal funds among the subjects of the Federation according to special criteria and formulas.

By 1996–97, the Russian model of budgetary federalism was firmly established. However, practically every one of its elements contains a potential for conflicts between the center and the regions, as well as between regions with varying status in the budgetary system.

Forms and Sources of Budget Conflicts

At the moment, conflicts between the center and the regions regarding taxation and budgetary issues do not present a real threat to the Russian state and its budget system. Today, only Tatarstan, Bashkortostan, and Yakutia can stop the transfer of taxes to the federal budget, as they have managed to "nationalize" the local branches of federal tax agencies and have been able to form a sufficiently autonomous budgetary and taxation system in general. However, the great majority of the subjects of the Federation do not have that capacity for several reasons:

- Taxes are collected by federal agencies—the State Taxation Service and the State Customs Committees—and all payments are supervised by the Central Bank and the Federal Treasury. Certainly, regional authorities can, and do, apply certain pressure on the territorial structures of these agencies. However, as a rule, this pressure is clearly insufficient to cause any significant disruption of the existing hierarchy;
- The federal center is capable of using purely financial methods to deal with any "tax disobedience" of separate subjects of the Federation. In one out of three subjects of the Federation, the volume of federal grants and transfers exceeds the volume of taxes paid by that region into the federal treasury. If we add to this the direct expenses from the federal budget for territory and

pension fund subsidies, then the number of such regions more than doubles. For the few "donor" regions, any open conflict with the federal center might be associated with equally serious financial losses, for example, an outflow or bank capital;

- Contrary to widespread opinion, it is not the regions that are "paying" taxes to the center; the federal authorities are actually sending a part of their taxes to the regions. This circumstance becomes a more and more important argument against any legal argument for non-payment of federal taxes; and
- Under the present circumstances, a threat of non-payment of taxes on the part of this or that region would be perceived as an attempt to destabilize an already complex situation. As such, it is doubtful that such an attempt would find support among either the population at large or a majority of the national elite.

All this gives us reason to believe that, at the moment, the probability of a subject region ceasing to transfer taxes to the federal budget fund is no more than theoretical. Among other things, this is confirmed by the fact that, even at the height of the crisis of 1991–93, there were only four republics that did not pay federal taxes (Chechnya, Tatarstan, Bashkortostan, and Yakutia) and three of these rushed to settle their relationship with the federal budget office immediately after the situation stabilized. Moreover, even during the holdout of 1996, the State Tax Service collected 54 billion rubles in Chechnya, almost 10 percent of which were transferred to the federal treasury.

Except for these republics, there were no cases of suspension of transfers of federal taxes. In August and September of 1993, about 30 regions declared that they would stop tax payments, but none of them acted on that threat. In 1996, St. Petersburg resorted to a similar action, but even that rather influential subject of the Federation was only able to stop the transfer of 20 percent of its land-use tax to the federal budget (which is a local, not federal, tax, a portion of which is to be transferred to the federal authorities according to an existing agreement with the regions).

Looking ahead, the prospect of an escalation of the tax and budgetary conflicts between the center and the regions is limited by the following two circumstances, at minimum:

- Laws on taxation and budget issues are subject to obligatory approval by the Council of the Federation; i.e., by representatives of the regions. The regional lobby is rather well represented in the State *Duma*, as well. Therefore, most meaningful issues are agreed upon while laws are still being reviewed by the Federal Assembly.

- Financial agencies of the subjects of the Federation, cities, and regions are still under dual control, supervised by both regional (local) authorities and by the Ministry of Finance. In this situation, local financial officials can instigate open conflict with their own ministries only under strong administrative pressure by regional authorities, who are generally in a weak position.

As a result, almost all actual budget conflicts between the center and the regions are settled inside the "corridors of power." Overt actions (in the form of political statements, documents and declarations or even the initiation of legal proceedings) are usually taken in order to back up positions in the unofficial bargaining process with federal authorities. Though resorting to such demonstrative acts in itself signifies a rather serious crisis in the relations between the center and a region, we should not overestimate the real influence of such acts on the final decision-making process.

Current Conflicts

The basic issues around which there are currently budget conflicts between the center and the regions are:

- the asymmetry of the country's budgetary system;
- the division of income and expenses between different levels of the budgetary system; and
- the distribution of financial aid to the regions.

At the present stage of development of the Russian model of budgetary federalism, the attention paid to these problems in the form of overt or covert bargaining activities between the Federation and its subjects and any other search for compromises is a positive factor. Thanks to such conflicts (certainly, in their "civilized" form), the budget system of the country is being reformed in accordance with the requirements of real federalism.

Asymmetry of the Budget System

Constitutional Status. It is widely believed that the national groups (republics and "autonomous") are privileged in comparison with their "Russian" counterparts. Budgetary statistics, in fact, show that the republics indeed have a higher level of spending per capita, that they retain a higher portion of collected tax revenues, and that a larger portion of their income comes from federal sources. This contrast is even more obvious if we look at the "poor" autonomous regions (excluding the oil-producing Khanty-Mansijsky and Yamalo-Nenetsky territories). *(See Table 3.1.)*

Table 3.1

Various Subjects of the Federation With Different Constitutional Status in 1996*

	Budget Expenses Per Capita (in thousands of rubles)	Share of Federal Aid in the Budget as Expenses (in percents)	Share of Federal Taxes Credited to the Subject's Budget (in percents)
Per subject of the Russian Federation, on average	1536	11.7	56.8
Republics	1750	17.9	70.1
Krais, oblasts	1242	12.7	61.0
Federal cities	2635	3.9	44.4
Independent *okrugs, oblasts*	6525	5.9	50.0
Including "poor" areas	2878	42.3	74.2

Here and further - data for first nine months of 1996.

SOURCE: Calculations performed by the author based on data provided by the Ministry of Finance and by the State Taxation Service of the Russian Federation.

Some of these distinctions are explained by objective factors. For example, the majority of independent *okrugs* are underdeveloped areas located in the Northern and Eastern regions of the country. In these cases, the combination of high expenses and extreme dependency on the federal center seems quite predictable. In the same manner, among the republics there are more underdeveloped and/or geographically "costly" regions.

At the same time, a "subjective" factor apparently also affects the budget numbers. As a rule, the republics have a higher level of budget expenses paid for by infusions from the federal budget (either as direct transfers or as permissions to retain the majority of tax revenues collected in the republic) than the "Russian" subjects of the Federation with comparable conditions and levels of development. *(See Table 3.2.)*

Table 3.2

Various Subjects of the Federation in Different Geographic Regions in 1996

	Per Capita Budget Expenses (in thousands of rubles)	Share of Federal Aid in the Budget as Expenses (in percents)	Share of Federal Taxes Credited to the Subject's Budget (in percents)
European North:			
Republic of Karelia	1860	20.0	76.6
Republic of Komi	2458	7.0	57.7
Arkhangelsk *oblast*	1209	10.8	70.3
Vologda *oblast*	1413	7.3	76.0
Murmansk *oblast*	1676	14.5	67.3
Middle Volga:			
Republic of Mordovia	1543	39.5	59.4
Republic of Mary El	1404	26.6	61.4
Chuvashi Republic	973	21.2	63.3
Republic of Tatarstan	1892	1.1	80.3
Nizhniy Novgorod *oblast*	1178	5.9	51.1
Penza *oblast*	787	30.9	63.9
Ulyanovsk *oblast*	989	14.0	60.2
Lower Volga:			
Republic of Kalmykia	1955	65.5	44.9
Astrakhan *oblast*	1126	33.6	58.2
Preuralye:			
Republic of Udmurtia	1353	12.2	64.1
Kirov *oblast*	949	26.1	64.6
Perm *oblast*	1291	3.5	56.5
Southern Ural:			
Bashkortostan	1884	2.5	71.9
Orenburg *oblast*	1225	11.0	62.3
Chelyabinsk *oblast*	1408	4.0	71.0
South of West Siberia:			
Republic of Altai	1470	60.1	60.3
Altai *Krai*	1157	33.6	67.8
Transbaikal Region:			
Republic of Buryatia	1659	33.2	68.7
Chita *oblast:*	1149	19.3	67.7
Far East:			
Republic of Sakha (Yakutia)	4697	28.1	70.8
Magadan *oblast*	3936	32.2	68.0

SOURCE: Calculations performed by the author based on data provided by the Ministry of Finance and by the State Taxation Service of the Russian Federation.

Thus, there are reasons to believe that, up to the present time, the constitutional status of formally equal (in rights) subjects of the Federation differs; that republics really do occupy a more advantageous position in the budgetary system than *krais* and *oblasts*. However, this is only an external manifestation of deeper asymmetries in the current Russian model of budget federalism.

Special Agreements. In 1991–93, Tatarstan, Bashkortostan, and Sakha (Yakutia) practically ceased sending tax payments to the center. In 1994 and 1995, these republics signed agreements with the Federation regarding the division of authority, including agreements on taxation and budget issues. Under these agreements, these republics acquired a special budgetary status. In essence, they were freed from paying certain federal taxes in return for their agreement to finance a portion of the federal expenses in their territories. *(See Table 3.3.)*

Table 3.3

The Portion of Taxes Credited to the Budgets of "Privileged" Republics in 1992-1996 as a Percentage of Total Taxes Collected in Each Republic's Territory

Republic	Year				
	1992	**1993**	**1994**	**1995**	**1996**
Tatarstan	99.9	100.0	83.8	77.3	80.3
Bashkortostan	99.9	100.0	87.5	73.8	71.9
Yakutia (Sakha)	98.8	99.8	100.0	99.5	70.8
RF Subjects, on Average	48.3	62.9	64.8	59.1	57.3

SOURCE: Calculations performed by the author based on data provided by the State Taxation Service of the Russian Federation.

Any damage inflicted on the budget system of Russia by the special status of Tatarstan, Bashkortostan, and Yakutia is political and legal, not fiscal, in character. Individual exceptions to general rules in themselves create constant pressure on the budgetary system, slow down the reform of inter-budgetary relations, and discredit federal legislation.

For example, the signing of the agreement between the federal center and Bashkortostan caused fierce protest from the Perm *oblast*. The Legislative Assembly of the *oblast* demanded the establishment of real equality among the various subjects of the Federation. Subsequently, this demand was repeatedly raised by large "donor" regions (Sverdlovsk *oblast*, Krasnoyarsk *oblast*, the city of St. Petersburg, and others). As a result, "special agreements" began to be concluded with "Russian" subjects of the Federation, thereby mitigating some conflicts in the budgetary system but creating others.

Many of the agreements that were signed in 1995–96 do not provide any tax and budget privileges to the regions signing them (for example, Kabardino-Balkaria, Northern Ossetia, Buryatia, Orenburg *oblast*). Others, however, contain provisions or codicils that grant the regions quite sizable authority and financial resources (Udmurtia, Republic of Komi, Sverdlovsk and Nizhniy Novgorod *oblasts*, Krasnodar *krai*, etc.).

As a rule, the agreements between the center and regions provide that a portion of federal taxes collected in the region will be directed toward the financing of federal expenses and programs within the territory of that region. Federal tax monies are not credited to the budget of the region but are utilized directly by territorial branches (agencies) of the Federal Treasury. The greatest benefit of such "mutual credit" accrues to the financially strong regions, where the sum of the collected federal taxes appreciably exceeds the obligations of the federal budget to the enterprises and population in the region. In this case the regional authorities have an opportunity to indirectly control significant cash flows. At the same time, this arrangement also makes sense for the federal fiscal authorities: clearance time is reduced; regional authorities are motivated to collect not only their own local, but also federal, taxes; and the responsibility for the financing of federal expenses is partially assigned to the regions. However, there are negative consequences, as well:

- Deciding which regions will be allowed to participate in such arrangements becomes a source of political tension.
- The implementation of these arrangements remains virtually unregulated. Everything depends on the specific agreements reached between the federal and regional authorities. This causes a tug-of-war, or undeclared competition, between regions, which destabilizes the entire budgetary system.
- Regional authorities are encouraged to act according to the principle: "You do not finance your expenses on our territory, and we in turn do not transfer our taxes to you." Sometimes this principle is directly stipulated by the agreement. For example, Sverdlovsk *oblast* reserved its right to keep a part of the federal taxes it collects in the event that the federal government does not carry out its budgetary obligations to local enterprises and organizations.
- Finally, and this is perhaps the most dangerous factor, regional authorities could begin to perform intermediary functions between the federal center and local enterprises, organizations, and populations, determining the terms and (depending on their influence within the territorial branches of the Federal Treasury) amounts of their financing, as well as the terms for financing various federal expenses. It is possible that as the next step, the authorities of financially strong regions could appropriate the majority of federal responsibilities, which, under unfavorable circumstances, could cause a new spiral of conflict between the center and the regions.

Regional Tax Experiments. Various tax experiments that were introduced by presidential or governmental decree in a number of the Federation's subject territories are a further form of budget asymmetry.

From 1992–94, such an experiment was conducted in Karelia. That republic was given the right to credit to its budget 90 percent of all federal taxes collected in its territory. Those funds were listed as a "tax credit" and were directed to a fund for the development and reconstruction of the republic. During this period, Karelia (just like the three republics that led the "Parade of Sovereignties") actually enjoyed special budgetary status. In 1995, the republic returned to the common budget format; however, the issue of bringing back the "tax credits" has remained unresolved.

In 1994, by resolution of Russian Federation's government, a special "Favorable Economic Zone" was created in the territory of Ingushetia. Enterprises registered there were exempt from federal taxes, and the republic was given a tax credit for those amounts. The Ingush experiment is seen in two very different ways. The leaders of the Republic hail its expediency and point to all the social and industrial projects funded by the federal money. The Ministry of Finance and the State Tax Service are critical of the idea, accusing financial and commercial entities that participated in the creation of the "zone" of tax evasion and the "laundering" of illegal income. However, it is impossible to judge the experiment from a purely fiscal point of view, since it stemmed from a desire to form a belt of regions politically loyal to the federal center around Chechnya. We should view the agreements regarding the division of authority signed between Kabardino-Balkaria and Northern Ossetia from the same point of view, as well as the granting of the special status of "Free Economic Zone" to Dagestan, Kabardino-Balkaria, and Karachaevo-Cherkessia (purely nominal, so far), and so on.

The creation of Ingushetia's Favorable Economic Zone brought noticeable pressure upon the country's budget system. On the one hand, other underdeveloped regions demanded similar privileges; on the other hand, authorities of a number of regions began to protest against the outflow of major taxpayers to the Economic Zones. Stavropol *krai* suffered from such an outflow, leading the Stavropol *Krai Duma* to adopt a special resolution in March 1995 demanding that the federal authorities stop the experiment in Ingushetia. That demand was not met, but Stavropol *krai* was granted special tax benefits. This is a typical way of resolving a conflict over budget asymmetry: regions whose leaders very actively protest against the inequality between the subjects of the Federation are often granted certain special benefits, after which the issue is considered resolved until further protests occur.

Ways to Minimize Conflicts Stemming from the Asymmetry of the Budgetary System. Federal authorities still lack a clear position on the asymmetry of Russia's budgetary system. Protests on these grounds (usually by Russian "donor" regions) were either left unanswered or were dealt with through ad hoc, behind-the-scenes negotiations, resulting in the signing of inter-budgetary agreements with the most influential among the Federation's subjects. As a result, budget inequality among the subjects of the Federation increased, but the protests became less and less audible as a constantly growing number of regions received various privileges.

The Russian Federation, with its huge territory and dramatic internal contrasts, will likely be unable to avoid a certain asymmetry of the budgetary system. However, such asymmetry should be accompanied by rigid restrictions guaranteeing complete "transparency" of tax and budget relations between the federal center and the subjects of the federation.

First of all, it is necessary to resolve a basic question: whether "special" budget forms are acceptable in the Russian model of budgetary federalism. In the case of a positive answer, these arrangements should be legalized by federal legislation and not by separate agreements. A negative answer assumes that federal legislation should directly and explicitly forbid introducing any regional exceptions into a standard structure of inter-budgetary relations.

Both these alternatives are far from ideal. In the first case, Russia's budgetary system would become excessively complex and, as a consequence, difficult to manage. The second variation might promote conflict between the center and "privileged" republics and, in the long term, other financially strong regions.

The distinctions between subjects of the Federation in terms of population, size, and economic and financial potential present weighty arguments in favor of at least some differentiation between budgetary regimes. For example, exceptions could be made for regions that are capable (after fulfilling their obligations to the federal treasury) of receiving a higher degree of budgetary independence and responsibility. Similarly, exceptions could be made for underdeveloped or poorly developed regions that depend completely on federal assistance. However, *these should be exceptions*. The standard budget system, which should combine an optimal degree of budgetary independence and federal financial guarantees, should be the one most "convenient" for the majority of regions. All requirements for exceptional budget status should be stipulated in detail in federal legislation and rigorously observed.

The exclusion from the general structure of inter-budget relations of regions that, for objective reasons, are not capable of independently formulating their own budgets would offer an opportunity to optimize the distribution of federal assistance and to strengthen the budgetary independence of the majority of the Federation's subjects. At the same time, "special" budget agreements enjoyed by Tatarstan, Bashkortostan, and Yakutia could gradually be incorporated into the budgetary regime that is created for financially strong regions. Suggestions to this effect are already being put forth by the leadership of Russian "donor" regions, and it makes sense for the federal authorities to lead this process and to establish in advance a clear legal framework. Otherwise, the suggestions of "donor" regions might take the form of unacceptable demands on the federal budget. In order to become a way of preventing conflicts between the center and the regions, rather than a source of such conflicts, workable elements of budget asymmetry should have a precise legislative foundation.

Division of Income and Expenses Between the Different Levels of the Budgetary System

These traditional problems of inter-budget relationships have prompted a greater degree of conflict in Russia than in other countries because of incomplete budgetary system reform, political and economic instability, and the lack of a reconciliation mechanism to coordinate interactions between authorities at different levels.

Division of Budget Expenses. The financing of social programs, social security, and capital investments has been transferred to the regional subjects of the Federation. At the same time, there is no federal legislation regulating the division of authority and responsibility between the center and the regions. Throughout the budget year, decisions are made at the federal level (for example, regarding increasing the minimum wage) which impose additional financial obligations on the regions. Though federal legislation contains a clause regarding compensation for such charges, it is not enforced in practice. For example, a dramatic conflict was caused by the adoption in 1995 (on the initiative of the Federal Assembly) of a federal law, "On Veterans," which was to be funded in part by the regional budgets. As no additional funds were allocated for implementation of that law, a number of regions refused to pay for its implementation, and others introduced only some of the benefits stipulated by that law. On the other hand, because of uncertainty in the division of budgetary responsibility, regional authorities frequently aspire to shift the full responsibility for financing local budgetary expenditures onto the federal budget. For example, demands to pay back wages to state employees are, as a rule, addressed to the federal government, even though to a large extent it is regional and local budgets that are responsible for those debts.

Division of Budgetary Income. At the present time, Russia has a very decentralized budgetary system. Although at the end of the 1980s the regions were estimated to receive less than 40 percent of the budget's allocations, by 1996 they received around 50 percent—and, in terms of percentage of tax revenues, almost 60 percent. *(See Table 3.4.)*

Table 3.4

Russian Federation Subjects' Budgets as Percentages of the Income Category of the Consolidated Budget of the Russian Federation in 1992–1996

	Year				
	1992	**1993**	**1994**	**1995**	**1996**
Total Income (without Inter-Budgetary Transfers)	44.1	49.5	51.1	49.0	51.0
Tax Revenues	48.3	62.9	64.8	59.1	55.8
Including:					
Profit Tax	58.7	67.6	64.9	64.9	68.4
Income Tax	100.0	100.0	99.4	91.1	90.7
VAT	24.9	35.7	36.4	29.0	35.1
Excise Tax	52.5	49.6	40.0	27.0	18.5

NOTE: Calculations performed by the author based on data provided by the Ministry of Finance and by the State Taxation Service of the Russian Federation.

By these indices, Russia does not fall behind and even outperforms a majority of federations. For example, in Australia, the states receive only 20 percent of tax revenues; in the United States, 45 percent; and in Canada, about 50 percent. Unlike in these countries, however, the division of budget income between federal and regional budgets in Russia occurs spontaneously in many respects, reflecting political calculations and the balance of forces within the corridors of power. Neither a federal tax code nor federal tax laws regulate the distribution of taxes to the different levels of the budget system. This problem is solved by an annual law on the federal budget.

In the past few years, under conditions when 70-80 percent of the subjects' tax revenues have taken the form of deductions from the federal tax base, the struggle for division of tax benefits between the center and the regions has become one of the most characteristic features of the budget process. This struggle was especially dramatic during the period of 1991 through 1993. Besides the aforementioned "tax wars," it manifested itself in the annual (and in 1992, even quarterly) revision of allowed levels of deductions transferred from federal tax revenues to regional budgets. Just as during the Soviet period, these deductions were differentiated by the regions. For example, in 1993 some of the regions, under the pretext of reducing inter-budgetary flow, were allowed to retain 50 percent of the value added tax (VAT) collected in their territories, while other, more developed regions kept 20 percent. This created a latent conflict between the center and the regions, as well as between subjects of the federation belonging to different groups. Things improved in 1994, thanks to the introduction of uniform specifications regarding the amounts that be deducted from federal taxes and transferred to the budgets of the regions. As a result, the struggle now revolves around the establishment of a standard method of dividing these taxes, which is inherently better than a competition to get individual privileges from the center.

From 1992-94, income tax revenues were allocated entirely to the subjects of the federation. In 1995-96, 10 percent of that tax was credited to the federal budget. Although that 10 percent was still being used in the regions to finance housing and social infrastructure projects, which were transferred to local authorities, the regional governments were highly critical of this change. Additionally, in 1994-96, various subjects of the Federation made the demand/offer to retain up to 70 percent of the total sum of taxes collected in the regions in local budgets. Lately, the most common demand has been to keep 20-25 percent of the customs duties, all of which today go into federal coffers. Making concession to the regions' desire to stabilize inter-budgetary relations, the federal government, in the "Law on the Federal Budget for the Year 1996," established criteria for federal budget allocations to the regional budgets for 1996–98.

Regional and Local Taxes. The law entitled, "Regarding the Basis of the Tax System of the Russian Federation," which was adopted in 1991, specified a comprehensive list of taxes that regional and local authorities had the right to introduce. However, at the end of 1993, all limitations were lifted by a presidential decree. As a result, from 1994 to 1996, subjects of the Federation and local bodies of authority began actively to form their own tax systems. Instead of being based on the usual variety of taxes and fees of a "local" nature (annoying the taxpayers not by their rates, but by their number), these tax systems were often analogs to the federal system and practically destroyed the tax base of the country.

Belgorod *oblast* introduced regional export and import duties, an excise tax, an additional income tax, and a profit tax for banks. Sales taxes and various "special-purpose" taxes to support unprofitable industries (mostly agriculture) were widely introduced. Tax barriers for imports—in contradiction to the Constitution of the Russian Federation—appeared. Nevertheless, although the Ministry of Finance and the State Tax Service stepped forward from time to time with rather sharp criticism of regional tax-writing, they did not take any outright measures to limit that process.

It is possible that some of the federal government's passivity was due to the preparation of a 1996 draft Tax Code that restored the specific lists of regional and local taxes. Even though it is still unclear whether that law is going to be adopted (due in part to resistance from the regional lobby), a step in the same, right direction has also been taken through an August 1996 Presidential decree canceling the "tax freedom" of the regions beginning January 1, 1997. Regional and local authorities were asked to cancel taxes not specified by the federal law "Regarding the Basis of the Taxation System in Russia."

Ways of Conflict Resolution. Just as with the asymmetry of the budget system, the prevention and resolution of conflicts in the realm of the division of revenues and expenditures between different levels of the budget system depend upon creating a stable legal foundation. In regard to the accounting powers of federal, regional, and local bodies of authority and management, federal laws—or a section of a more general budget law—should be adopted, ensuring absolute clarity ("transparency") about these kinds of inter-budgetary relationships. At the same time, it is necessary to create specific mechanisms that will prevent the imposition of additional expenses (not supported by income sources) on the budgets of lower levels. (Such a requirement exists in federal law, but it is virtually unenforced.)

As to the division of tax revenues, it is strategically important to increase the role of regional and local taxes. Thus, there will be a combination of three universally accepted approaches: introduction of "parallel" taxes, which go to federal, regional, or local budgets; division of revenues from national taxes among different levels of the budget system; and use of varying rates for the same taxes by federal, regional, and local authorities.

Distribution of Financial Assistance to the Regions

Distribution of financial assistance to the regions is one of the most painful problems for any federation. Even in politically and economically stable states this issue sparks intense discussion, and sometimes even conflict.

The Fund for Financial Support of the Regions (FFPR). Since 1994, a Fund for Financial Support of the Regions (FFPR) has existed within the federal budget. Its funds (which have been given the name *transfers*) are distributed among the "needy" and "especially needy" regions in accordance with special formulas. Introduction of a formula for the distribution of federal assistance has not caused any major resistance from the subjects of the Federation. Apparently, after a rather rough period from 1991–93, regional authorities realized that it was necessary to practice at least some restraint regarding the covert struggle over depleted budget resources.

The federal government has established more rigid guidelines for regulating the financial appetites of the regions. Although the FFPR has been increased every year, annual federal budgets have clearly specified the total sum allocated for all the regions. For 1996-98 this allocation was fixed at 15 percent of federal tax revenues. As a result, the attempts of some regions to get a larger portion of the FFPR not only meet resistance from the federal government, but also from other regions worried that their shares of the fund will diminish.

The formula for distribution of federal assistance has been a subject of sharp and, as a rule, well-grounded criticism. However, no alternative to that formula has yet been suggested. Due to this, all conflicts regarding the formula have shifted toward arguing about how to apply it. First, conflicts arise over the criteria for selecting "needy" and "very needy" regions. To calculate the regions' share of the FFPR, the government uses their financial statements and income and expense declarations. This information is coordinated annually between the Ministry of Finance of the Russian Federation and each region, and then adjusted for the upcoming fiscal year. Given the absence of any regulation of this process, the unreliability of financial reporting, and the manipulation of the adjustment process (done, for example, by using additional budget income and expense categories) there is wide variation in the results. With adequate persistence, the authorities of practically any region have the opportunity to dramatically increase their share of the FFPR (at the expense of less assertive, or less influential, regions).

Another issue for argument is how the transfers are issued. Presently, the Ministry of Finance uses two methods: a) allocation of transfer payments directly from federal budget funds ("direct" transfers); and b) allocation of transfers by increasing the VAT rate for the "needy" regions ("indirect" transfers). In 1995, "direct" transfers comprised 74 percent of FFPR transfers; "indirect," 26 percent. Depending on the regions, these proportions could vary rather widely. *(See Table 3.5.)*

When the tax base is stable, it is better for the regions to receive "indirect" transfers, rather than to wait until the funds come in from the federal government. When taxes are difficult to collect, though, it is preferable to shift the responsibility for the transfers to the federal authorities.

Table 3.5

The Share of "Direct" and "Indirect" Transfer Payments for Some Subjects of the Federation in 1995

Subject of the Federation	"Direct" Transfers	"Indirect" Transfers
Volgograd *oblast*	100	0
Vologda *oblast*	97	3
Novgorod *oblast*	86	14
Pskov *oblast*	63	37
Republic Maryi-El	56	44
Republic of Mordovia	50	50
Chelyabinsk *oblast*	43	57
Novosibirsk *oblast*	38	62

SOURCE: Calculations performed by the author based on data provided by the Ministry of Finance of the Russian Federation.

Finally, the terms of transfers also present a potential source of conflict. Usually, all regions receive the funds allocated to them by the end of the year (proportional to the degree of fulfillment of the federal budget); however, parameters of current fulfillment of the plan, as a rule, vary significantly depending on a number of subjective factors. *(See Table 3.6.)*

Thus, even the most formal aspect of the mechanism of rendering financial assistance to the regions abounds with numerous subjective elements. On the one hand, interruptions in continuity create preconditions for conflicts between the center and the regions. On the other hand, some space for maneuvering promotes the adaptation of inter-budget relationships to new regulating principles. The regions that are especially dissatisfied with the formula for transfer distribution have an opportunity to increase their shares of the FFPR. The regions which fail to increase their shares might set up more convenient delivery systems for transfers or expedite their allocation. As a result, we see a certain compromise between the requirements of "classic" budget federalism and the actual ability of the budgetary system to implement those requirements.

Table 3.6

Fulfillment of the Transfer Allocation Plan for Ten Months of 1996 (in percents)

Subject	Percentage of Plan Fulfilled
Vologda *oblast*	100
Kostroma *oblast*	73
Chelyabinsk *oblast*	69
Khabarovsk *Krai*	63
Ulyanovsk *oblast*	60
Krasnodar *Krai*	53
Voronezh *oblast*	52
Astrakhan *oblast*	50
Republic of Khakassia	47
Ivanovo *oblast*	39
Volgograd *oblast*	37
Average: RF	58

SOURCE: Calculations performed by the author based on data provided by the Ministry of Finance of the Russian Federation.

Other Types of Financial Assistance to Regions. Besides FFPR transfers, the federal budget also has several categories from which the regions receive additional funds. Together, they form 30-35 percent of the total volume of financial assistance to the regions. Two of them—financing of social projects and housing (transferred to the local authorities) and subsidies for importing agricultural products to the regions of the Far North—are not classified according to region. Accordingly, the regional authorities keep fighting for them throughout the year. Moreover, every year the federal budget allocates funds to finance regional development programs. An attachment to the federal budget specifies which regions will receive money from this category. Decisions are based on presidential and governmental decrees pertaining to regional issues. However, criteria for inclusion on this list, substantiation of allocated funds, control mechanisms for their use, and estimates of efficiency for the financed projects remain hidden in the depths of the budgetary process. A similar situation takes place when grants and subsidies are distributed from the federal highway fund, as well as subsidies to administrative and territorial entities.

One more potential source of conflict is that of subsidies granted to Moscow to perform the "functions of a capital city." In the last two to three years, Moscow, which is now the "richest" subject of the Federation, has been receiving about five percent of the total volume of federal aid to the regions. In their present form, these capital-city subventions are the results not of economic expediency, but of the political influence of Moscow's government not only with the federal government, but in the majority of other regions. It is not really surprising that other subjects of the Federation, who are desperately battling for each ruble of the federal grants, are rather indulgent regarding annual allocations to Moscow of what must seem to them to be huge amounts of funds. The most active protests against these "capital" subventions are usually voiced in the State *Duma* by deputies from St. Petersburg. However, their criticism results at best in insignificant reductions of funds requested by Moscow and put into the draft of the federal budget proposal.

Mutual Settlements and Loans. Within the budget process, there is a significant flow of funds between the center and the regions whose volumes and direction are not regulated by any legislative acts, including the annual federal budget laws. The main informal channel of financial support of the subjects of Federation is the so-called "mutual budget settlement." In 1994, 48 percent of the total volume of financial aid to the regions went through this channel; in 1995, 24 percent; in the first nine months of 1996, 20 percent. Reducing the proportion of mutual settlements is a positive process which reflects the increasing "formalization" of inter-budgetary relations, although in a normal budgetary system such settlements should not exist at all.

Funds received by the regions as a result of mutual settlements can be divided into several categories: adjustments to the budget (compensation for additional expenses or reduction in income during the fiscal year); financing of federal programs through the regional budgets; repayment of debts of the federal budget, etc. All of them are determined for individual regions in a process of ongoing negotiations and coordination with the Ministry of Finance. The results, as in other informal financial relations, depend on the power and influence of the regional authorities.

The same can be said about short-term loans offered by the federal government. In 1996, as the result of a campaign to pay back-wages, the regions received ten trillion rubles worth of these loans, which was equal to two-thirds of the FFPR. Also, if the share of the FFPR was calculated for each region according to a specific (though far from perfect) method, distribution of short-term loans among the regions was done without clear criteria or procedures.

Ways to Reduce Conflicts When Distributing Financial Assistance to the Regions. The best method to reduce conflicts in this aspect of inter-budgetary relations is through formalization and diversification: first, formalize ways of granting financial assistance to the regions, which would reduce opportunities for ad hoc bargaining practices; and second, diversify by attaching different regions to various channels for obtaining federal assistance, thus altering the position of regional authorities in their relationships to the federal treasury. In general, the mechanism of distributing financial assistance to the regions might involve the replacement of the federal budget fund (or the creation within it) by a minimum of three special-purpose funds for support of the regions, each having its own rules and distribution criteria:

1) A Grant Fund. This is an analog of the present support fund, but with a more effective method of distribution based on a comparison of the budgetary needs and tax potentials of the regions. 30–35 regions in the most difficult financial positions should receive grants from this fund.
2) A Subvention Fund. Unlike grants, subventions are given for very specific purposes. These funds should be distributed separately, on the basis of competition among an unlimited number of regions (in various proportions), for every expense category (education, health care, social security, subsidies for socially important areas of the economy, transfers of housing previously owned by large enterprises to the local authorities, etc.).
3) A Regional Development Fund. The distribution of this fund could be in the form of subventions only for investment purposes (mainly for social and industrial infrastructure development), awarded partially according to formulas and partially on the basis of bid tenders for projects and programs.

It would hardly be possible to completely remove elements of subjectivity from this area. Moreover, that would be dangerous, as it would deprive these inter-budgetary relationships of a certain flexibility which is needed during the period of transition. However, it is necessary to put these elements into a more precise legal framework. The following principle should become a general rule: what can and must be discussed are distribution criteria, mechanisms, and procedures that are uniform for all of the Federation subjects, *not* the specific amounts or conditions of individual grants or transfers.

"Donors" and "Recipients." "Donor" regions are interested in reducing the territorial redistribution of budget resources; decentralizing control of budget expenditures, and, especially, revenues; acquiring "special" budget status; creating their own tax services; removing their financial agencies from the control of the Russian Ministry of Finance; becoming more independent in issuing securities, etc. The interests of "recipient" regions are directly contradictory. It makes no sense for them to seek greater budgetary independence, since the weakness of their own tax bases and the overloading of their budgets with social obligations moots the very idea of their acquiring "free" financial resources. That is why they are, in general, willing to settle for centralization of the tax system in return for increased financial support to their regions.

The relationship of taxes collected in the regions to the existing budget expenditures of the subjects of the Federation can be used to determine whether a particular region is designated as a "donor" or "recipient" (this does not apply to republics with "special" budget status). For example, for the regions where this parameter is lower than 0.6, even the total amount of taxes collected in their territories would cover only 60 percent of their existing expenses. That is why they will be the most staunch supporters of preserving or even increasing centralization of tax revenues, since this will ensure them a greater portion of the funds collected among the main "donor" regions. "Donors" are the regions where local tax potential exceeds budgeted expenses by more than 1.5. *(See Table 3.7.)*

Table 3.7

Types of Regions According to Coverage of Budget Expenditures by Their Tax Potential, 1996

Type of Region	Coverage	Subjects of Federation (in decreasing order of coverage)
"Donors"	More than 1.5	Moscow, Khanty-Mansijsky Autonomous *oblast*, Sverdlovsk, Samara, Perm, Nizhegorodskaya, Moscow *oblasts*, Yamalo-Nenetsky Autonomous *oblast*, Ryazan *oblast*.
"Conditional Donors "	1.3 –1.5	St.-Petersburg, Chelyabinsk *oblast*, Krasnoyarsk *Krai*, Tomsk, Leningrad, Yaroslavl, Belgorod, Novosibirsk, Irkutsk, Omsk, Kaluga, Volgograd, Tver, Ulyanovsk *oblasts*, Krasnodar *krai*, Udmurtia, Orenburg, Tula *oblast*.
"Intermediary"	1.0 –1.3	Smolensk, Vladimir, Saratov *oblasts*, Stavropol *Krai*, Republic of Komi, Bryansk, Voronezh, Tyumen, Rostov *oblasts*, Khabarovsk *Krai*, Nenetsk Autonomous Okrug, Penza, Lipetsk, Kemerovo, Vologda *oblasts*, Primorye Territory, Kaliningrad, Murmansk, Kirov, Chita *oblasts*, Chuvashi *oblasts*.
"Conditional Recipients"	0.6 –1.0	Arkhangelsk, Kurgan, Sakhalin, Tambov, Amur, Astrakhan, Kostroma, Kamchatka, Pskov area, Altai Territory, Karachaevo-Cherkessia, Adygea. Karelia, Taimyrr AO, Buryatia, Magadan area.
"Recipients"	Less than 0.6	Ingushetia, Jewish Autonomous *oblast*, Mordovia, Komi-Pemyatsky AO, Kabardino-Balkaria, Maryj El, Kalmykia, Republic of Altai, Chukotka AO, Northern Ossetia, Ust-Ordynsky Buryatsky AO, Tuva, Evenk AO, Dagestan, Koryak, Aginsky Buryatsky AO, Chechnya.

SOURCE: Calculations performed by the author based on data provided by the Ministry of Finance and by the State Taxation Service of the Russian Federation.

The influence of the authorities in regions with varying budget situations can be evaluated with the help of Table 3.8 (*see below*).

Table 3.8

Regions with Varying Budget Situations

	Seats in the Council of the Federation	Percentage Share of the Federal Budget	Voters (percents)	Voted for the CPRF in 1995 (percents)	Voted for Yeltsin in 1996 (percents)
"Donors"	18	55.4	23.6	17.0	66.8
"Conditional Donors"	36	21.2	28.9	20.8	51.8
"Intermediate"	52	15.2	27.8	26.3	46.4
"Conditional Recipients"	32	4.0	9.5	25.5	46.6
"Recipients"	34	1.2	4.5	27.7	54.7
"Special" Structures	6	3.0	5.6	20.8	56.7

SOURCE: Calculations performed by the author based on data provided by the Ministry of Finance and by the Central Election Committee of the Russian Federation.

The financial power of the "donor" regions is supported by the steady pro-reform orientation of their electorate. At the same time, they have fewer seats in the Federation Council than the more highly subsidized and, as a rule, more anti-reform regions. What stands out is the disproportionately high representation of the "recipient" regions (in relation to their population and their input into the federal budget). As demonstrated by the outcome of 1995–96 elections, the conservative orientation of their population can, if necessary, be quite successfully reoriented toward support for the federal center.

For the federal and regional elite such a ratio opens a rather wide field for various maneuvers and combinations regarding inter-budgetary relations between the center and the regions.

Conclusion

Thus, the current atmosphere of tax and budget conflicts between the center and the regions is characterized by the following peculiarities:

- Stabilization of the political situation and relative strengthening of the federal center in comparison with the period of 1991–93 have sharply lowered the threat of tax and budget separatism and its most acute manifestation, the cessation of tax payments to the federal government.

- The asymmetry of Russia's budget system, as one of the forms of prevention of budget conflicts between the center and financially strong regions, creates constant tension in the budget system. To prevent the occurrence of conflicts it is less important to realign the budget status of the regions than to legitimize budgetary asymmetry on the basis of clear legislation.
- Particularly at the present stage of the strengthening of Russia's budgetary federalism, problems regarding dividing budget expenditures and revenues and distributing federal aid remain a source of elevated tension. The reasons for this are both objective conflicts between the center and regions and an excessively broad arena of informal struggle over budget resources.
- Direct representation of the regions in the Federation Council, on the one hand, and the centralization in the organization of tax and budget systems remaining from the Soviet system, on the other hand, limit the scope of open conflicts between the center and regions. The majority of these conflicts are being resolved by informal negotiations and coordination of interests within the framework of various administrative and power structures.

The probability of aggravation of budget conflicts between the center and the regions under the present circumstances is insignificant. A return to the situation of 1991–93, including displays of tax and budgetary separatism on the part of financially strong regions, is possible only in the event of a dramatic destabilization of the political and economic situation in the country. In that case, budget conflicts would unavoidably become a consequence or manifestation of a system-wide crisis, but not its cause.

In order to gradually reduce conflicts in the tax and budget sphere, it is necessary to move from "experimental" to "legislative and regulatory" budgetary federalism. This should be based on the Tax Code, the revised Law on Budget Systems and Budget Processes, laws regulating relationships between various levels of the budget system, and laws regulating the financial basis for local self-governance as well as social and financial norms.

At the same time, the formalization and streamlining of inter-budget relationships and their inclusion in a rigid legal framework should not outpace a more general process of the evolution of Russian federalism and the overcoming of economic crisis. Otherwise, the federal center might lose the opportunity for compromises with regional authorities. Now that it is increasingly possible that political and, especially, economic instability will increase, such hastiness might prevent the ironing out of conflicts regarding redistribution of the potentially depleted resources of the national budget system and, instead, aggravate such conflicts.

4. Ethno-Political Change in the North Caucasus

Larisa L. Khoperskaya[*]

Introduction

The announcement of the "Declaration on the State Sovereignty of the Russian Federation" marked a new stage of Russian history—a stage full of stormy political events and an intensive search for ways to reform the national-state system of the Russian Federation. In the Northern Caucasus, various models of statehood have been adopted, ranging from the Adygei to the Chechen versions. The model chosen depended on the pro- or anti-Russian orientation of the local authorities. Hence, it is already possible to identify certain regularities of development in the Northern Caucasus region:

- in the transitional period (from the Soviet to the post-Soviet society) the ethno-social factors came to the fore and politics acquired an ethno-political character;
- as a result of the crisis of government and rebirth of an ethnic consciousness, the most socially and politically active groups proved to be ethnic groups, on which the social structure of the population of the Northern Caucasus was based;
- new political actors have appeared. Various ethnic elites have created institutions which effectively express the political interests of their ethnic constituencies and usurp the role of governmental structures;
- the entire system of managing ethnic and national processes has changed, from top to bottom;
- the need to coordinate the interests of various and competing ethnic groups has led to a variety of competing and often contradictory ethnic policies, advocacy of which has become the distinguishing trait of various political powers;

---

[*] The author is head of the Rostov-on-Don Bureau of the North Caucasus Department of the Ministry of Nationalities of the Russian Federation.

- the historical memory of ethnic groups has turned out to be a significant factor in political life, with historical arguments becoming a major component of political debates;
- real federalism and confederalism have become issues on the agendas not only of official governmental structures, but of unofficial but highly organized ethnic movements; and
- ethnic and nationalistic separatism left the area of theory and entered the sphere of political reality.

Ethnic Movements and the Formation of a New Political-Legal Order

Between 1990 and 1996, the formation of politicized national movements with their own ideas about reforming the national-state system in the North Caucasus was completed. Projects for the division, or federalization, of the republics (Daghestan, Kabardino-Balkaria, Karachai-Cherkess) in accordance with ethnic principles were put forward, as well as projects for the creation of a two-chamber legislature with equal representation of the primary ethnicities of the republics in one of the chambers. The initiators of these processes were the political opponents of the incumbent republic authorities, i.e., the ethnic movements.

Thus, in Daghestan the Kumyk movement ("Tenglik") demanded creation of a Kumyk state, while a Nogai organization ("Birlik") demanded autonomy for the Nogai people; the Lezgin movement ("Sadval") threatened to create an independent state if Russia did not grant the Lezginis autonomy in a Dagestani federation; and the Tersk Cossacks declared their secession from the republic.

In Kabardino-Balkaria the Balkar national movement demanded the formation of a Federal Republic of Kabarda and Balkaria in which the minority Balkars would enjoy both full equality and virtually complete autonomy. Later, the Kabardanian and the Balkarian movements went even further and agreed to the dissolution of the Kabardino-Balkarian Republic—an agreement that was supported by the Supreme Soviet of the Kabardino-Balkarian Republic. Meanwhile, the republic's Russian-speaking population, first and foremost the Cossack assembly, began to agitate either to secede from the Kabardino-Balkarian Republic and join the Stavropol *krai* or to remain in the Kabardino-Balkarian Republic as an equal and autonomous subject of the Kabardino-Balkarian Federal Republic. All of this created an enormously unstable ethno-political situation in the region.

The greatest contradictions engendered by the efforts of ethnic movements to obtain a legal-constitutional status occurred in the Karachai-Cherkess Republic, where five ethnicities demanded recognition as "full subjects" of the federation. While the Karachai, the Cherkess, and the Cossack movements cited the fact that their peoples had earlier had their own forms of statehood, which should now be reestablished, the Abazin and the Nogai movements demanded the *de novo* creation of their own ethnic districts.

It is notable that, regardless of ethnic specifics, all of these movements went through the following stages of development:

- the creation of an organization (e.g., "Adyge Khase," "Tenglik," Birlik," Cossack Circle," etc.) which proclaimed ethnic-cultural rebirth as its aim;
- the establishment by these organizations of political parties dedicated to changing the state system, enforcing the claims of their constituents to their "historic" land, to property that had been confiscated as a result of deportation, and/or to financial compensation for past deprivations; and
- the consolidation of ethnic community and political organizations in order to take over the government and to carry out the full range of governmental functions.

As a result of the activity of the ethnic movements in the region the political and legal status of ethnic groups won official recognition as a debatable issue. This became clear as early as November 1992 at the Congress of the Peoples of Daghestan, which was convened under the aegis of the republic's incumbent ruling elite. This recognition, in turn, determined subsequent developments: the ethnic movements shifted from active opposition to collaboration with reformed organs of government, while the latter appropriated many of the slogans of their former opponents. The dialogue, which began between the authorities and the ethnic elite, was reflected in the evaluation of the situation by the population of the region. *(See Table 4.1.)*[1]

---

[1] Here and further are summations of the results of sociological surveys which were conducted, under the direction of the author, by the personnel of the Laboratory of Regional Management of the Northern Caucasus Academy of State Service in 1995–96. During a mass survey based on a quota selection, 1,484 respondents were questioned in the republics of the Northern Caucasus and the Rostov region. The selection is representative in terms of ethnicity, sex, and age. During the conduct of an expert survey, 183 members of the region's political-administrative elite were used as experts. The percentages shown in the tables is that of the total number of respondents.

Table 4.1

How Has the Republic's Declaration of Sovereignty Affected the Political Interests of Ethnic Groups?

	Region: Population (in percents)						
	Adygei	Daghestan	Ingushetia	Kabardino-Balkaria	Karachai-Cherkess	North Ossetia-Alania	Rostov Region
Improved	36.23	40.17	47.24	40.30	38.13	34.97	15.64
Deteriorated	12.32	28.61	24.41	21.39	28.13	25.17	36.02
No Change	45.65	30.35	22.05	30.35	32.50	30.77	22.27
Undecided	5.80	0.87	6.30	7.96	1.25	9.09	26.07
Total:	100.00	100.00	100.00	100.00	100.00	100.00	100.00

The enhanced political status of ethnic groups on the federal level raised the authority of the ethnic movements, political parties, and social organizations of the Northern Caucasus among local residents and led to a qualitative change in the character of their activity. This was expressed in the mass mobilization of the entire population and its grassroots differentiation along ethno-political lines. In a relatively short time, three basic attitude sets emerged: pro-Russian, anti-Russian, and pan-ethnic regionalist.

In addition, federal authorities began to recognize the leaders of ethnic movements as legitimate interlocutors on behalf of their constituents in political negotiations. An early case in point was a meeting convened on the initiative of the Supreme Soviet and the State Ethnic Committee of the Russian Federation in Pyatagorsk in January 1993. Although the unambiguously pro-Russian orientation of the meeting precluded the participation of the representatives of the Chechen republic, the representatives of 93 North Caucasian social organizations participated, and many of them signed the meeting's final act, the "Declaration on the Principles of Inter-Ethnic Relations in North Caucasus," which gave important (though insufficient) impetus to negotiations to end the Ossetian-Ingush conflict which was raging at the time.

Although the leaders of many of the ethnic movements in the region favored the creation of mono-ethnic states, the incumbent ruling elite was far less radical. *(See Table 4.2.)*

Table 4.2

Do You Support the Creation of Ethnic States?

	Region: Administrative/Political Elite (in percents)					
	Summary	Adygei	Daghestan	Ingushetia	Kabardino-Balkaria	Rostov Region, Krasnodor Territory
Yes	6.01	0.00	3.85	11.36	2.86	16.67
No	73.77	74.19	82.69	59.09	82.86	72.22
Undecided	20.22	25.81	13.46	29.54	14.29	11.12
Total:	100.00	100.00	100.00	100.00	100.00	100.00

In the event, moreover, moderation prevailed. Although the constitutions adopted by the North Caucasian republics in 1996 claim sovereignty on the basis of the right of ethnic groups to political self-determination, they also claim to express the will not only of the ethnic majority but of all resident ethnic groups, thereby providing ethnic minorities with a constitutionally guaranteed status. The legal status of ethnic minorities is explicitly guaranteed, for example, in the constitution of Daghestan: "The Republic of Daghestan guarantees the rights of indigenous peoples and ethnic minorities in accordance with generally accepted principles and provisions of international laws and international agreements. Each of the ethnicities of Daghestan is guaranteed equal rights to the defense of their life interests on a constitutional basis." Elsewhere, constitutional references to "indigenous peoples," "ethnic minorities," "peoples constituting the republic," and "historically formed community of peoples, living on its territories" leave no doubt about the acceptance of the concept of ethnic rights.

The acceptance of ethnic groups as subjects of political and legal rights on the republican level has been accompanied by the development of the mechanisms for realizing these rights in practice. Among such mechanisms are:

- the creation of national districts for indigenous ethnic groups in districts where they are compactly settled;
- establishment of quantitative and qualitative norms for the representation of given ethnic groups in republic organs of government;
- a requirement for fluency in both the indigenous and Russian languages as a condition for high office in the republic governments;
- demarcation of the rights and of republican bodies and ethnic movements in managing ethnic processes;

- creation of a system of reciprocal restraint among ethno-political elites (the creation of inter-ethnic movements, the integration of ethnic minorities into the official structures of authority, the blocking but not the destruction of extremist ethnic groupings, etc., and;
- mobilization of institutions of customary law (councils of elders) and religion as regulators of inter-ethnic relations.

In this manner, in the Northern Caucus republics, the focus of policy has become the regulation of relations between the state (represented by republican authorities) and the various ethnic groups.

The animating force behind this policy has been the acceptance of the legal status of ethnic groups, through the introduction of constitutional provisions for their representation in the highest organs of authority. For example, the principle of equal representation of the Adygei and the Russian-speaking populations in the executive and legislative organs of the republic is enshrined in the Constitution of Adygei. In the Constitution of Daghestan there are provisions for equal representation of the indigenous peoples of Daghestan in the executive branch; and for proportional representation in the legislature. In Kabardino-Balkaria, introduction of a two-chamber parliament with equal representation of indigenous ethnicities in one of the chambers is being discussed.

The significance of ethnic representation for both the general population and the political elite was once again confirmed by the result of sociological surveys conducted in 1995–96 by the Laboratory of Regional Management of the Northern Caucasus Academy of State Service. *(See Table 4.3.)* Ethnic representation in both the legislative and executive bodies turned out to enhance feelings of satisfaction among the majority of the region's population. *(See Tables 4.4, 4.5, and 4.6.)* It is interesting that the opinions of both surveyed groups (the population and the elite) corresponded on this issue.

Table 4.3

Are the Various Peoples of the Republic Equitably Represented in the Legislative Organs of Authority?

	Region: Population (in percents)						
	Adygei	Daghestan	Ingushetia	Kabardino-Balkaria	Karachai-Cherkess	North Ossetia-Alania	Rostov Region
Yes	54.35	37.86	62.99	55.22	50.00	55.24	29.38
No	22.46	28.61	24.41	20.40	25.63	20.98	11.85
Against Ethnic Representation	14.49	13.87	3.94	5.97	4.38	6.99	10.43
Undecided	8.69	19.66	8.66	18.41	20.00	16.78	38.34
Total:	100.00	100.00	100.00	100.00	100.00	100.00	100.00

Table 4.4

Are the Various Peoples of the Republic Equitably Represented in the Executive Organs of Authority?

	Region: Population (in percents)						
	Adygei	Daghestan	Ingushetia	Kabardino-Balkaria	Karachai-Cherkess	North Ossetia-Alania	Rostov Region
Yes	53.62	34.97	59.84	50.75	43.75	53.15	25.59
No	21.74	30.92	22.83	22.89	32.50	21.68	11.37
Against Ethnic Representation	13.04	13.01	3.94	7.46	4.38	6.99	12.32
Undecided	15.21	12.10	13.39	18.91	19.38	18.18	40.71
Total:	100.00	100.00	100.00	100.00	100.00	100.00	100.00

Table 4.5

Are the Various Peoples of the Republic Equitably Represented in the Legislative Organs of Authority?

	Region: Administrative/Political Elite (in percents)					
	Summary	Adygei	Daghestan	Ingushetia	Kabardino-Balkaria	Rostov Region, Krasnodar Territory
Yes	57.92	67.74	38.46	59.09	62.86	88.89
No	19.67	25.81	42.31	2.27	11.43	0.00
Against Ethnic Representation	11.48	0.00	7.69	20.45	17.14	11.11
Undecided	10.92	6.46	11.54	18.19	8.57	0.00
Total:	100.00	100.00	100.00	100.00	100.00	100.00

Table 4.6

Are the Various Peoples of the Republic Equitably Represented in the Executive Organs of Authority?

	Region: Administrative/Political Elite (in percents)					
	Summary	Adygei	Daghestan	Ingushetia	Kabardino-Balkaria	Rostov Region, Krasnodar Territory
Yes	51.91	77.42	17.31	52.27	68.57	77.78
No	22.95	12.90	63.46	2.27	8.57	0.00
Against Ethnic Representation	14.21	0.00	7.69	29.55	17.14	16.67
Undecided	10.93	9.68	11.54	15.91	5.71	5.56
Total:	100.00	100.00	100.00	100.00	100.00	100.00

At present, the acceptance of a legal status for ethnicities is being debated by the center and the republics as an effective means for stabilizing inter-ethnic relations. This status can only be realized, however, through the development of a solid legal base, which, in turn, depends on the highest legislative and executive organs of government. Today the legal bases in the republics of the Northern Caucasus and in the center are markedly different—a situation which considerably retards the realization of ethnic stability.

Ethnic Self-Consciousness and Conflict

Along with the stabilizing aspects, the aspiration of ethnic groups toward a legal status (in the extreme case, a mono-ethnic state) is utilized by ethnic elites and by some representatives of the federal government as a "wild card" in national politics. This can be seen in *Table 4.7*.

Table 4.7

To What Extent Do Regional Authorities Take Into Consideration the Interests of Ethnic Groups?

	Region: Administrative/Political Elite (in percents)					
	Summary	Adygei	Daghestan	Ingushetia	Kabardino-Balkaria	Rostov Region, Krasnodar Territory
To a large extent	21.31	29.03	28.85	18.18	17.14	5.55
Not significantly	37.16	41.94	21.15	56.82	37.14	33.33
Not at all	10.38	3.23	7.69	13.64	22.86	0.00
Undecided	15.30	16.13	15.38	11.36	8.57	33.33

The government of the Russian Federation must keep pace with the process of lower-level ethno-political reform and give ethno-political aspirations legal recognition. In particular, the mutual rights and claims of various ethnic groups need legal recognition. Otherwise, the inequality of rights of ethnic minorities will continue, leading, as today, to the expulsion of Russians or their exclusion from prestigious positions and consequent exodus of the Russian-speaking population from the Northern Caucasus.

Ignoring the ethno-political situation in the Russian Federation, and underestimating the strength of aspirations for ethnic self-preservation and self-determination can destroy Russian statehood itself, since denying the non-Russians the right to a political-legal status within the boundaries of a unified nation will rekindle and feed the flame of radical ethnic separatism. In the case of the Russians of the Northern Caucasus republics, the result can only be an upsurge of nationalism.